LEON KIRCHNER

TRIPTYCH

for Violin and Cello

AMP-8035

First Printing: April 1992

ASSOCIATED MUSIC PUBLISHERS, Inc.

Distributed by
 Hal Leonard Publishing Corporation
7777 West Bluemound Road P.O. Box 13819 Milwaukee, WI 53213

The first movement of this work may be performed separately under the title *For Cello Solo.*

Triptych was premiered on August 17, 1988 by Lynn Chang, violin and Yo-Yo Ma, cello at the Tanglewood Festival.

duration: ca. 20 minutes

TRIPTYCH
I. For Cello Solo
for Carter and Yo-Yo

Leon Kirchner
(1986)

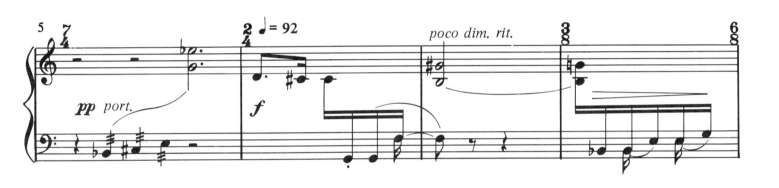

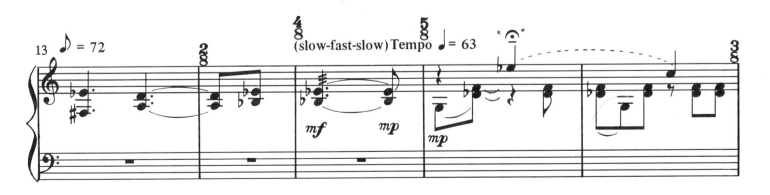

A tempo (move ahead a little)

poco a poco accel. e cresc. . . .poco a poco

* the violinist should enter (from offstage) playing this harmonic (in unison with the cello). The fermata should be held until the violinist has entered and is in place on stage.

II. For Violin and Cello Obligato

for Lynn and Yo-Yo

LEON KIRCHNER

TRIPTYCH

for Violin and Cello

AMP-8035

First Printing: April 1992

ASSOCIATED MUSIC PUBLISHERS, Inc.

Distributed by
Hal Leonard Publishing Corporation
7777 West Bluemound Road P.O. Box 13819 Milwaukee, WI 53213

The first movement of this work may be performed separately under the title *For Cello Solo.*

Triptych was premiered on August 17, 1988 by Lynn Chang, violin and Yo-Yo Ma, cello at the Tanglewood Festival.

duration: ca. 20 minutes

TRIPTYCH
I. For Cello Solo
for Carter and Yo-Yo

Leon Kirchner
(1986)

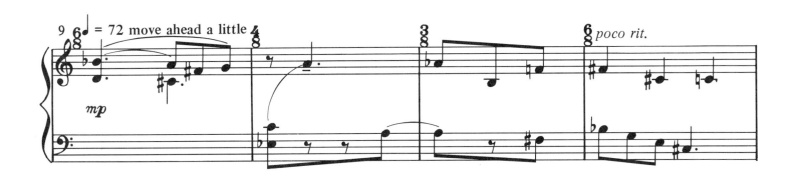

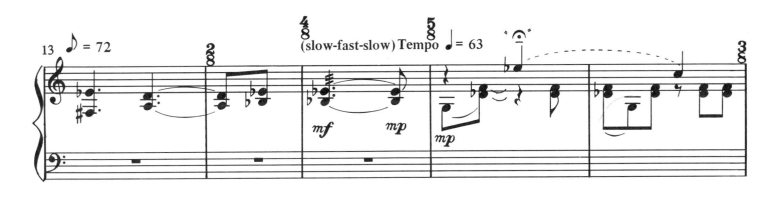

A tempo (move ahead a little)

* the violinist should enter (from offstage) playing this harmonic (in unison with the cello). The fermata should be held until the violinist has entered and is in place on stage.

12

II. For Violin and Cello Obligato
for Lynn and Yo-Yo

III.

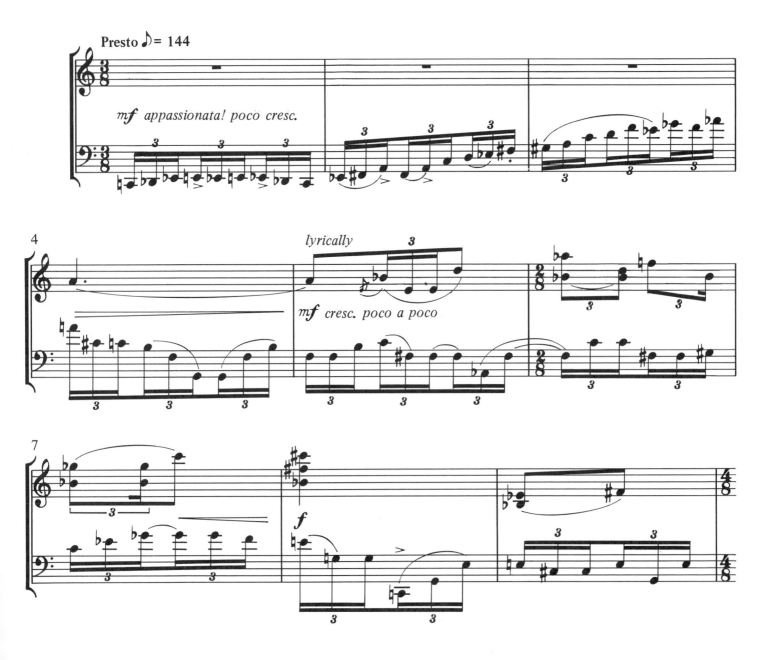

22

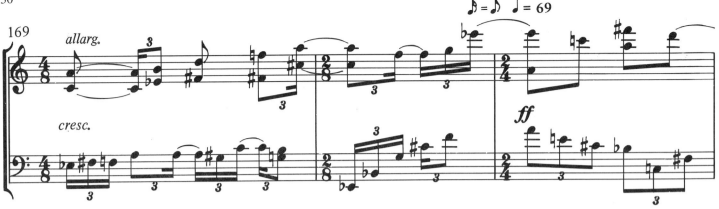

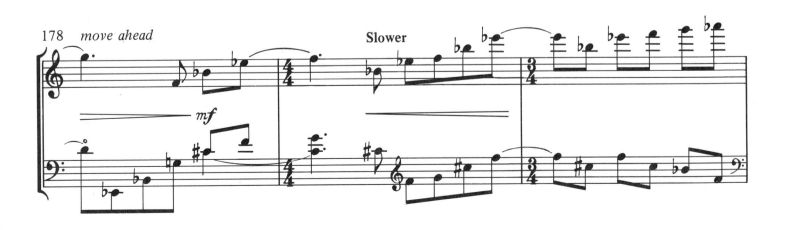

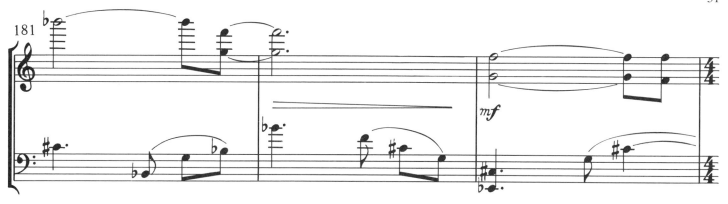

III.

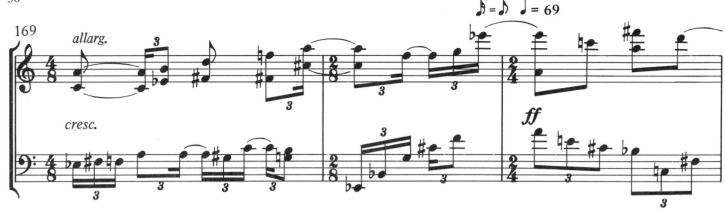

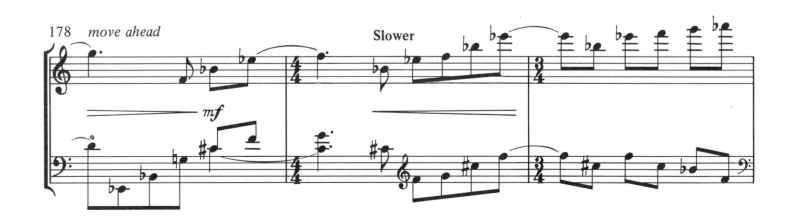

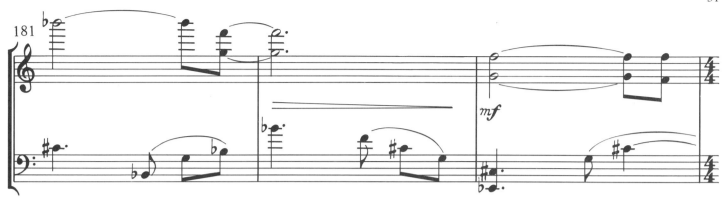